I0620379

Serenity Family

"A Journey of Friendship and Kindness"

Written, illustrated, and published by **Mona Mason**

Serenity Family

Copyright © [2024] by **Mona Mason**

All rights reserved. This book may not be used or reproduced in any way, whether it be graphic, electronic, or mechanical, photocopying, recording, taping, or by including through information storage and retrieval, system without the author's express written consent, with the exception of small quotes included in reviews and critical articles.

For permissions requests, contact:

Writersway Solutions, LLC

10685 Hazelhurst Dr STE B #38295

Houston, Texas 77043, USA

www.writerswaysolutions.com

1-888-666-4258

This work is fiction. Names, characters, places, and incidents are the author's imagination and are fictitious. Any resemblance to actual persons, living or dead, business establishments, events, or locales is entirely coincidental. All rights reserved. Please do not participate in or encourage piracy of copyrighted materials in violation of the author's rights. Purchase only authorized editions. No part of this book may be reproduced, scanned, or distributed in any printed or electronic form without written permission from the writer, Mona Mason.

ISBN (Paperback): 978-1-962733-38-0

ISBN (Hardback): 978-1-962733-39-7

ISBN (Ebook): 978-1-962733-37-3

Printed in the United States of America

Dedication

First, I want to give thanks to my Lord and Savior, Jesus Christ, for His unending love and guidance in all things. A special thanks to my loving husband, Timothy Mason, for your unwavering support, patience, encouragement, and endless love. You've carried me when I couldn't carry myself, and for that, I am forever grateful. To all the incredible children: Remember, it's okay to be different. You are loved just as you are. Show kindness, and if you or someone you know is being bullied, don't hesitate to tell a trusted adult. With love, Mona Mason

About This Book

Serenity Family is a touching story of friendship, resilience, and inclusion. Faith, who is biracial, struggled to find acceptance in her early years; she didn't look like any of the other children at daycare or kindergarten. Elijah, who has ADHD, often felt isolated because others saw him as different. Both found a special bond in each other, drawing strength from their friendship. As they grow, they learn that true friendship embraces each person's uniqueness. This story teaches young readers the power of empathy, the importance of standing up for one another, and the joy of creating a world where everyone, no matter their background or abilities, belongs.

Acknowledgment

I would like to express my deepest gratitude to Dr. Allen of Olive Branch, Missisipi, MD, Renee Reichert psychiatrist in Olive Branch, MS, and my Licensed Clinical Social Worker, Julia Wright of Olive Branch, Missisipi. Their guidance and support, along with the encouragement of my husband, Timothy Mason, gave me the courage to write Serenity Family as part of my healing process. I am grateful to them for helping me stop being embarrassed about my childhood past and for encouraging me to tell my story.

Additionally, thank you to Otis Amos and Kenneth Roberson for giving me resources and guidance along this journey. To the Dream Team and others at work who showed love and support upon my return to work. Thank you to all whose encouragement inspired me to write Serenity Family as part of my healing journey.

Appreciation

I would like to express my deepest gratitude to everyone who has supported me. Thank you to my parents, Martha and Clarence Johnson, for teaching me the value of hard work, respect, and faith. You gave me the strength to stand up for myself.

To my grandparents, Parthenia and Robert Watts, your home was always a safe place for me. I will forever cherish the love, wisdom, and protection you gave me. To my sister Marlo, brothers Clarence and Willie, and the rest of my relatives on Porter Bayou Road, thank you for being a part of the hilarious childhood memories we shared together. To my niece Crystal, caring for you when you were a child showed me that my calling was to work with children.

To the Mason family, thank you for accepting me as part of your family. Special thanks to Calvin and Renee Mason for always giving me a good laugh and listening ear. To Maurice and John Mason, your words of encouragement and wisdom helped me pursue my dreams. Thank you for reminding me that with faith and perseverance, anything is possible.

In a bright, cheerful town lived a girl named Faith, who was biracial with beautiful curly hair and green eyes that shimmered in the sunlight. She loved playground adventures, always accompanied by her best friend, Elijah, who had ADHD. Some days were hard for Elijah, and at times, the other kids didn't invite Faith and Elijah to play, making them feel lonely.

Faith and Elijah stood by each other, even when left out. They supported one another when bullies tried to push them off the swings, remaining strong and inseparable.

At daycare, they played fun games, built block towers, and enjoyed learning together.

As Faith and Elijah grew older and entered school, they embraced new friendships in a diverse environment with children from various backgrounds. Each morning, students enjoyed quiet time to pray or reflect, respecting each other's beliefs.

Mrs. Sharma, their teacher, greeted students warmly. She valued each child's uniqueness, creating an inclusive classroom where all children, including those with special needs, felt safe and valued.

Faith and Elijah soon made new friends. Faith especially loved joining them in snowball fights and playing games together.

Elijah sped down snowy hills with excitement. While both Faith and Elijah began to feel more accepted and found comfort in connecting with others who shared similar struggles, they started spending less time playing together.

Days passed, and Faith and Elijah found themselves spending less time together, engrossed in their new friendships.

Faith and Elijah started to miss each other. Though they occasionally exchanged waves across the playground, their friendship no longer felt the same.

Feeling lonely, Faith sat quietly on a bench, while Elijah found himself missing their playful games on the jungle gym.

10

Faith came up with an idea—she suggested to her friends that they all play together. The idea was met with excitement, and soon they were planning a winter play day, inviting everyone to join in the fun.

They eagerly prepared for the big day by creating invitations and organizing a gift exchange. Faith and Elijah secretly hoped to pick each other's names!

On the day of the event, the playground buzzed with laughter and excitement. Faith and Elijah were overjoyed to discover they had picked each other's names for the gift exchange.

13

During the games, they stumbled upon a shiny box buried in the snow. Inside, they discovered colorful friendship bracelets.

14

Excited by their discovery, Faith and Elijah shared the bracelets with everyone. Each child wore their bracelet proudly, spreading joy and serving as a reminder of the power of kindness.

15

Wearing their bracelets, the friends became a symbol of unity, bringing together old and new friends alike. Each bracelet represented the strength of kindness and the beauty of diversity."

As the sun set, some of the children held hands, embracing the warmth of friendship and unity. At 15, Faith and Elijah reflected on their growth, with friendships blossoming and their bracelets symbolizing kindness and unity. They felt ready for the next chapter of their lives.

Faith and Elijah invited everyone to come together, creating memories and building stronger bonds. As many prepared to graduate from 9th grade and move on to 10th grade at different schools, they reminded everyone that true friendship knows no color, each person is unique, and to always stand up for what is right while speaking out against what is wrong.

18

Faith, now mentoring younger students, reads them stories that promote respect, friendship, kindness, and the courage to speak up. She encourages children to share their feelings and to always tell a trusted adult if they experience or witness bullying.

As they graduated from junior high, Faith and Elijah looked back on their journey with pride. Through kindness and inclusion, they had created a ripple effect that inspired others. Their mission reminded everyone that even small acts of courage can make a big difference. Now, it's your turn to stand up, speak out, and make the world a kinder place."

Reflect and Discuss

1. What makes a good friend, and how can you show kindness to someone who is different from you?

2. How do Faith and Elijah's actions inspire you to include others?

3. What is one thing you can do today to make someone feel welcome?

About the Author

Mona Mason is passionate about helping children and giving back to her community. She holds an Associate's Degree in Child Development Technology from Northwest Community College, where she graduated at the top of her class and was recognized in Who's Who organizations.

She also earned a Bachelor's Degree in Social Work from the University of Mississippi, where she continued to excel academically. Mona has dedicated her life to caring for children, working as an Assistant Director of a daycare and later running her own daycare, Serenity Home Daycare, for five years. Her experience includes working for Child Protective Services, completing an internship at Regional One Health Burn Unit, and volunteering at House of Grace, a shelter for abused women and their children. Her inspiration for writing Serenity Family comes from witnessing abuse and her deep desire to teach children the importance of speaking up and telling a trusted adult if they are mistreated. Writing this book also played a significant role in her healing process, allowing her to confront and overcome past trauma. Mona's mission is to empower children to find their voice, embrace kindness, and celebrate diversity. She resides in Southaven, Mississippi, with her husband, Timothy Mason, and her support dog, Dango, who helps her manage PTSD. Mona dedicates this book to her daughter, Serenity, and all the children of the world, whose potential and dreams inspire her every day.

www.ingramcontent.com/pod-product-compliance
Lightning Source LLC
Chambersburg PA
CBHW041130120626
46547CB00019B/2935